100 ROCKABILLY LICKS FOR GUITAR

Master the Iconic Licks, Rhythms & Techniques of Rockabilly Guitar

DARREL HIGHAM

FUNDAMENTAL CHANGES

100 Rockabilly Licks For Guitar

Master the Iconic Licks, Rhythms & Techniques of Rockabilly Guitar

ISBN: 978-1-78933-218-6

Published by **www.fundamental-changes.com**

www.fundamental-changes.com

Over 11,000 fans on Facebook: **FundamentalChangesInGuitar**

Instagram: **FundamentalChanges**

For over 350 Free Guitar Lessons with Videos Check Out

www.fundamental-changes.com

Connect with Darrel:

https://darrelhigham.com

https://www.patreon.com/darrelhighammusic

Cover Image Copyright: Author photo, used by permission.

Contents

Introduction

Rockabilly: The Music

Rockabilly is the name given to the melting pot of styles that emerged as one of the earliest offshoots of Rock 'n' Roll music in the early 1950s. Rock 'n' Roll had emerged in the US during the late 1940s, and itself was a mixture of Blues and Country – specifically Rhythm & Blues and Western Swing. It wasn't labelled "Rock 'n' Roll" until the mid-50s.

The term Rockabilly is a mash-up of the words "rock" and the slightly derogatory "hillbilly". The phrase was adopted to describe this new musical offshoot, which many consider to be the purest form of Rock 'n' Roll. Rockabilly is a joyful music, with driving, infectious rhythms and characteristically dynamic guitar work. It has a particular feel, but more importantly a specific *sound* all its own. There is nothing quite like it and once you get hooked on the sound, you realise that it's about more than just music – it's a lifestyle.

In 1954, Elvis Presley, along with Scotty Moore on lead guitar and Bill Black on double bass, recorded the single *That's Alright Mama/Blue Moon of Kentucky* for Sun Records in Memphis, and this is universally considered to be the first pure Rockabilly recording. Elvis sang with all the soulful inflections of a gospel singer, and even on these early recordings you can hear in Scotty Moore's guitar work, licks and fills that would define the Rockabilly guitar style. Scotty was heavily influenced by legendary Country thumb-pickers Chet Atkins and Merle Travis, as well as the Jazz stylings of players like Les Paul.

Scotty's use of the thumb-picking style, with Bill Black slapping his double bass strings and Elvis' forceful acoustic rhythm guitar, greatly helped fill out the songs, as there are no drums present on most of Elvis' Sun recordings. In hindsight, producer Sam Phillips' decision to not use a full band for Elvis' initial session at the studio can be seen as another defining moment in the creation of Rockabilly. Due to the local success of *That's Alright Mama* (it sold approximately 35,000 copies) it was decided to keep this minimal set up for most of the subsequent recordings Elvis made for the label. Also integral to the recording process was the use of slap-back echo, an effect developed by Phillips, which helped to create the unique sound that has endured to this day.

Elvis, Scotty and Bill toured the South non-stop for nearly two years and influenced many other musicians to embrace the new sound, including artists such as Buddy Holly and Eddie Cochran. Elsewhere, pioneers like Carl Perkins, Gene Vincent (with notable guitar player Cliff Gallup in his band) and others blazed a trail for the style with their own recordings and live performances in the aftermath of Elvis' influence.

So much more could be said about the origins of the style, but sadly this isn't a book on the history of Rockabilly! One thing is for sure, however: from the early 50s until now, though musical trends have come and gone (from synthesisers to big-hair guitar music and more), Rockabilly has never gone away. New voices have always emerged to carry the torch for this music, which continues to make an impact. From Brian Setzer, Mark Harman, Ray Cotton, to Paul Pigat, Carlo Edwards and many more, it is as popular today as it has ever been.

To really capture the vibe of Rockabilly, it's essential to hear the music. To help you discover more, I've put together a Spotify playlist of my essential Rockabilly tunes you must hear. Open the Spotify app, tap in the search box and the camera icon will appear in the top right. Tap on the camera icon and scan the code below and the playlist will be added to your library.

Rockabilly: The Players

There are so many great Rockabilly guitar players to discover who have influenced the style, from old-school to new – too many to mention them all here. Instead, I want to highlight the players who have influenced my own playing style the most.

Eddie Cochran

Without doubt, Eddie Cochran has had the greatest influence on my playing. Towards the end of the 50s, his classic tunes, *C'mon Everybody*, *Summertime Blues* and *Somethin' Else* captured the imagination of his generation. His music, his style and rebellious attitude, then his untimely death aged just 21, destined him for iconic status.

As a guitar player, Eddie had a strong, authoritative style with bags of attitude and energy, though not at the expense of skill and finesse. He had a distinctive, cutting guitar tone and played instantly memorable riffs and well-conceived melodic phrases. If you want to nail the art of phrasing, listen to Eddie! The aggression in Eddie's playing has always attracted me. He has a way of grabbing your attention with dynamic guitar licks, even if he's playing on a ballad.

Eddie experimented with the guitar to achieve his unique sound. He often tuned his whole guitar down a tone, so he could play in standard tuning, but get a low, open D note. This gave his riffs a distinctive low growl that couldn't be replicated without retuning (and also made it more difficult for me to work out how he played his guitar parts!)

Whereas some players would play exclusively single-note lines with a Jazz influence, Eddie would always opt for a powerful rhythmic approach, played with a lot of attack. In reality, he was a far better guitar player than his recordings suggest, but he realised that the music was mostly about the hook and the groove, so he minimised his guitar work to serve the music.

I was only 5 or 6 years old when I first heard Eddie's music. I was flicking through my mum and dad's record collection and stumbled across the album *Singin' to My Baby*. On the cover Eddie is holding a beautiful Gretsch 6120 and it would become my ambition to own one. (I fell in love with the guitar before I listened to the music). Although this album is not considered part of the classic Cochran era in terms of its songs, it's my favourite of his because you really get to hear his guitar playing. The opening track, *Sittin' in the Balcony*, has a wonderful guitar break in the middle and Eddie's tone and feel are spectacular. And listen to the explosive guitar solos on *Am I Blue* – absolutely tremendous! Do check out this album if you get a chance.

Cliff Gallup

Cliff played in Gene Vincent's band for just one year in 1956, but during that time he recorded 35 tracks with Vincent including his massive hit record *Be-Bop-A-Lula*. These tunes are still revered by Rockabilly fans, but

Cliff's influence as a guitar player extended well beyond the genre. He was an inventive and beautiful guitar player who, outside of Rockabilly, could play just like Chet Atkins.

The story goes that when Vincent's band first went into Owen Bradley's studio in Nashville, the producer Ken Nelson and Bradley had session musicians waiting in the wings, ready to step in if the band wasn't up to scratch. But when Cliff played the guitar solos on the classic tune *Race With the Devil*, everyone knew they wouldn't be needed. Guitar players agree that Gallup was a man ahead of his time and many of the licks he invented are permanent fixtures in rock vocabulary.

Scotty Moore

Scotty Moore is the Father of Rockabilly guitar playing and was a founding member of the Blue Moon Boys, comprising Scotty, bassist Bill Black and, of course, Elvis Presley. Sun Studios owner Sam Phillips introduced Elvis to Scotty, and in turn Scotty introduced Elvis to Bill – the rest is history. Scotty became Elvis' live and studio guitar player from 1954 to 1968.

Scotty himself says that on the early Elvis recordings he was just trying out ideas – trying to mix things up and "inventing" things on the spot. His playing style was a combination of thumb-picking Country and a few choice Jazz licks he'd learnt from players like Barney Kessel, Tal Farlow and Les Paul. These diverse elements combined to make his unique sound, which worked especially well as the backdrop to Elvis' energetic, gospel-infused vocals.

Grady Martin

Grady Martin is a lesser known name, but as a session guitarist he was a member of the Nashville A-Team (a nickname for the versatile, elite session players who backed the best-known artists of the 1950s through to early 1970s, and whose members included guitarists Chet Atkins and Hank Garland).

Grady played on hundreds of hit records – too many to list – and countless Rockabilly classics including all the Nashville recordings by Johnny Burnette & The Rock 'n' Roll Trio, Johnny Carroll, Don Woody, and Ronnie Self to name a few. Grady was also credited with discovering the effect of adding fuzz tone to the guitar when he recorded the part to the tune *Don't Worry* by Marty Robbins through a mixing desk with a faulty channel!

As a player, Grady was similar to Cliff Gallup in that he was a clever player who was able to come up with endless interesting and inventive melodies. He always seemed to know exactly what to play to create the perfect introduction to a song, and all his solos are melodic and beautifully constructed.

* * *

I hope you get as much enjoyment out of exploring this great music as I have over the years!

Darrel

Get the Audio

The audio files for this book are available to download for free from **www.fundamental-changes.com.** The link is in the top right-hand corner. Click on the "Guitar" link then simply select this book title from the drop-down menu and follow the instructions to get the audio.

We recommend that you download the files directly to your computer, not to your tablet, and extract them there before adding them to your media library. You can then put them onto your tablet, iPod or burn them to CD. On the download page there are instructions and we also provide technical support via the contact form.

For over 350 free guitar lessons with videos check out:

www.fundamental-changes.com

Over 11,000 fans on Facebook: **FundamentalChangesInGuitar**

Tag us for a share on Instagram: **FundamentalChanges**

Chapter One – Signature Licks

Like spoken languages, every genre of music has common phrases that are essential to know if want to become fluent and sound authentic. Like jazz or blues, Rockabilly also has *must-know* licks that you need to get under your fingers to capture its authentic sound and vibe. In this chapter I'm going to show you some single-line Rockabilly "signature licks" to get you started.

Attitude, feel and tone are just as important as the notes being played in this style of music, so be sure to download and listen to the audio examples for the licks before you play them.

Along the way, I'll explain any special techniques and theory you need to know, so that you have the tools to develop your own licks later. But a lot of Rockabilly follows the three-chord Rock 'n' Roll format, so the theory you need to know is minimal.

More so than most types of music, Rockabilly riffs and licks tend to be very closely linked to the chords over which they are played. The licks will often follow the chord shapes as they move around the neck. The first few examples here are based around a G major chord in third position.

Because Rockabilly bands invariably include an upright bass player, I tend to avoid playing root notes on the low E string, as indicated in the chord diagram below. The bass player is always playing the root in this style of music, and the rhythm guitar tends to play chords voiced on the top strings, so that they punch through the mix with the characteristic cutting Rockabilly tone.

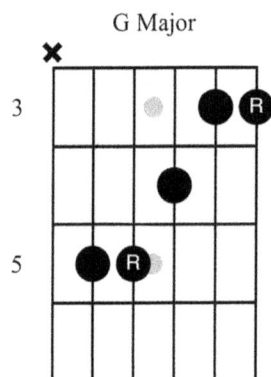

G Major

3

5

To solo over this chord, Rockabilly guitarists will freely mix and match major and minor pentatonic scales, much like a blues guitarist. Combining the two scales enables us to play in a single position on the fretboard, but at the same time have access to more note choices for licks.

This is illustrated in the diagrams below. The first diagram shows the G Major Pentatonic scale, and the second shows G Minor Pentatonic – both in third position. The third diagram is a hybrid shape that combines both scales into one. As we progress, you'll notice that many Rockabilly lines jump between major and minor tonalities, so it's useful to have this combined shape under your fingers, and to be aware of all the note options that are available.

G Major Pentatonic   G Minor Pentatonic   Combined Shape

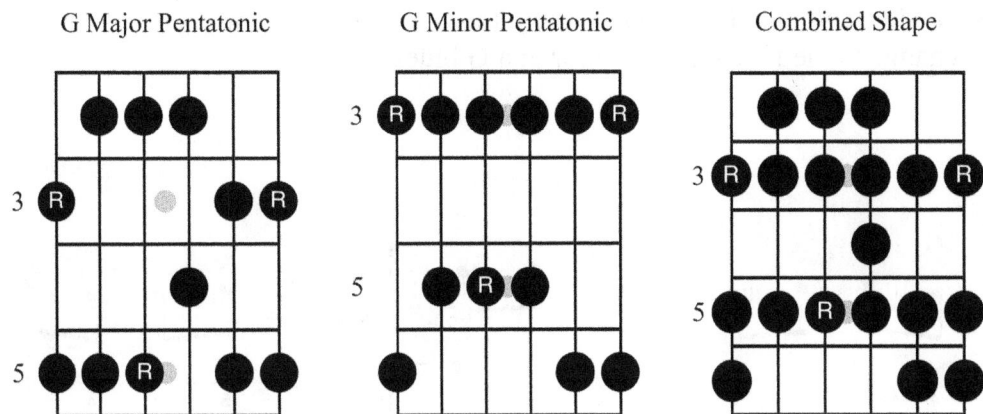

Our first example is as absolute staple Rockabilly lick. Although a clichéd blues lick on the face of it, it takes on a different feel when played with the classic Rockabilly tone and attitude. (See the chapter on Guitars, Amps & Effects at the end of the book for advice on equipment).

Example 1a

The next licks sneaks in an extra note that's not in our hybrid scale pattern (the Db note on the A string, fourth fret). This is a chromatic approach note. Using approach notes is a technique borrowed from Jazz, where we anticipate a chord tone by approaching it from a half step below or above. These non-scale tones provide a split second of tension that is quickly resolved and they add momentum to a line.

Example 1b

Here's a longer line that begins with the same bluesy cliché, then loops back on itself before extending the line.

To end the phrase, I add a common blues move where the G major chord shifts down to F major. This usually occurs before the change to the IV chord (C major in a G blues).

Example 1c

Here's a variation of the previous idea that breaks out of the third position chord/scale box to extend the lick up the fretboard. In bar three, I play a pedal tone idea to help ascend the neck.

In pedal tones, an open string is often used to play a repeating note, while other fretted notes are played against it. A lot of Rockabilly tunes are written in open-chord, guitar-friendly keys, so you'll often hear guitar breaks that include lines utilising the open high E string, like this one.

Example 1d

The next example combines two common Rockabilly techniques: double-stops and hammer-ons/pull-offs. To execute this lick, position your fretting hand as if you're going to hold down a G major chord. Barre the G and B strings at the third fret with your index finger and keep it in place while your ring finger does all the work. Play this lick using all downstrokes. After the double-stop, play the triplet figure using a hammer-on and pull-off, then hammer onto the G note on the D string, fifth fret.

Loop the first bar of this lick around multiple times to get it sounding nice and smooth. In bar two I end this line with a surprise major third (a B note).

Example 1e

Example 1f combines a few of the ideas we've seen so far. It begins as a single-note line, then moves into a double-stop riff.

Example 1f

The next example is another variation played in position three, using the combined major/minor pentatonic scale. Watch out for the fast triplet phrase played in bar four. Execute it with a quick hammer-on/pull-off.

Example 1g

Example 1h has a similar vibe to the previous lick, but notice that you can vary a lick and make it sound different by making slight alterations to the rhythm and the length of notes.

Example 1h

The next example is played over chord IV (C major) in a G blues. Any of the licks you've already learnt can be transposed and be played at the eighth fret instead of the third (based on the C major barre chord shape at the eighth fret). As an alternative to repeating a lick, we can outline the C major chord by playing a simple double-stop riff like the one in Example 1i.

Example 1i

The next three licks are ideas you can play as a blues progression turns around. In a G blues, the V chord (D major) is played before the progression resolves to the I chord (G major).

In Example 1j, play the fast slides in bar one with plenty of attitude and make them big!

Example 1j

The next example steals an idea from Country guitar playing – playing phrases in 6ths. If you play any note in the G Major scale, then walk up five more scale steps, the note you arrive at is a 6th interval away from the first note. For example, if we play a B note, the 6th interval will be a G:

B C D E F# **G**

You can invert this idea and walk *down* the scale too. Once you hear how this sounds, you'll recognise it immediately, as it's a feature of nearly all Country guitar solos.

Below is the G Major scale arranged in 6ths. The scale tones are placed on the high E string and the 6ths are located on the G string. (You'll always skip a string when playing in 6ths). 6ths can be played by plucking both notes simultaneously, but in Rockabilly it's more common to *displace* the notes (and easier if you're playing with a pick). Play through the pattern by picking the note on the G string first, followed by the note on the B string. E.g. B – G, C – A etc.

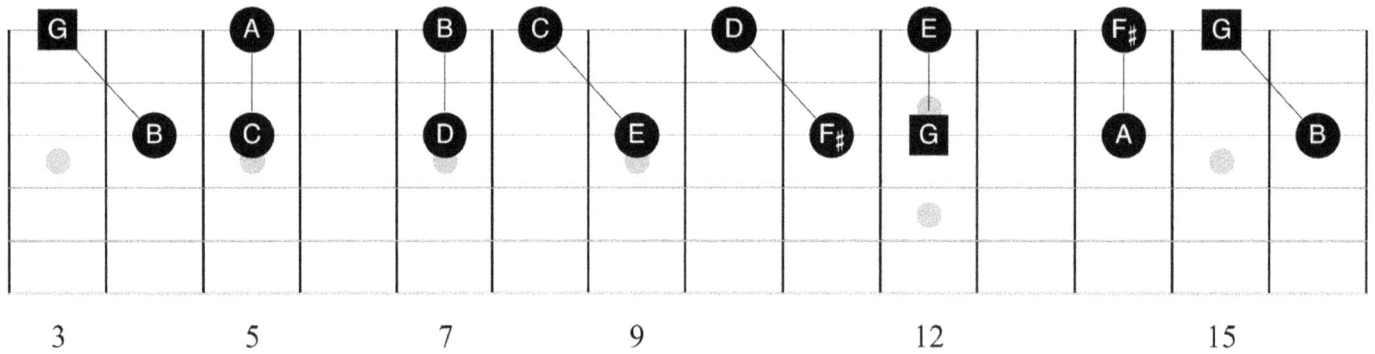

Now let's hear this idea incorporated into a lick. The 6ths are played over the D chord in bars 1-2.

Example 1k

Example 1l features a displaced octave pattern to outline the D major chord in bars 1-2. The idea here is that you play an octave shape, but don't hit the notes at the same time (as is common in Jazz). Instead, the lower note is played first, then the same note an octave higher is played a fraction later – just like the 6ths in the previous example. I'm also using a chromatic idea here, beginning on the D major chord, then ascending one fret at a time to fill out the bars.

Example 1l

So far, we played lots of licks based around position three, but of course we can play a G major chord in other places on the neck, and different chord shapes open up new ideas for vocabulary. The next few licks will be based around this G major chord in position seven:

Example 1m is played in free time and included here so you can explore this new position. Play it slowly and notice the notes that naturally fall under the fingers.

Example 1m

Bending notes is relatively rare in Rockabilly playing, but it is done occasionally for effect. Here's a lick in the higher position that starts with a bend.

Example 1n

To end this chapter, here's a full chorus of a blues in G that brings together some of the ideas we've looked at so far. The only potentially tricky part is in bars 8-9, where quick arpeggios spell out the sound of the chords. Play through the whole thing slowly to begin with and make sure you can play it cleanly before you attempt to play it up to tempo.

Example 1o

Chapter Two – Rhythm Chops

At its heart, Rockabilly music is all about the rhythm. A song might have a driving, straight-ahead Rock 'n' Roll feel, a bouncing Country feel, or a syncopated Swing feel – but they are all about the groove. It's important to lay a strong rhythmic foundation for this music, because at the end of the day, it's *dance music* and the audience needs to connect with that strong pulse.

Since the guitar is both the main harmonic and melodic instrument in Rockabilly, it's important to have good rhythm chops as well as being able to solo. In this chapter I'm going to show you the most common Rockabilly rhythms. This also means tackling one of the most important, but challenging rhythm techniques you need to know to master this style: *Travis picking*.

First, let's learn some common Rockabilly rhythm parts that don't rely on Travis picking.

Rock 'n' Roll-style Bassline Driven Rhythm

As an offshoot of Rock 'n' Roll, Rockabilly features similar driving rhythms. You'll instantly recognise many of these ideas, which were conceived and developed by the early pioneers of Rock 'n' Roll. In true Rockabilly style, these are played with lots of attitude in a no-nonsense manner. Because most Rockabilly bands comprise guitar, bass and drums, it's best to set your guitar to the bridge pickup to achieve a tone that cuts through the mix, occupying the midrange frequencies.

Many a beginner guitarist, when they learned their first barre chord, had a revelation when they discovered they could play *the* Rock 'n' Roll riff, just by moving their pinky finger two frets! This chugging rhythm has never gone away, so I include it here for completeness. Note that you don't need to hold down a full barre chord to play it, however. It works best with a root and 5th power chord. Here it is played on a C major chord.

Example 2a

Another common Rockabilly rhythm is achieved by approaching a standard barre chord from a half step below to create a riff. This was a feature of Eddie Cochran's style. Slide into the third fret C major chord from the second fret and keep the picking hand chugging rhythm consistent. Listen to the audio to capture the timing.

Example 2b

Another easy-to-play but effective approach is to hold down a chord and reach for an alternative bass note, without moving position. Here I'm holding down an open A chord at the second fret. I'm barring it with the index finger to free up the middle finger, which can then access the G bass note on the low E string, third fret. This riff bounces between the A and G bass notes to create a strong accompaniment.

Example 2c

Example 2d demonstrates how to apply this idea to all the chords in a blues in A Major to create a classic driving rhythm part. This time I'm playing with a straight rhythm, rather than swinging it.

Example 2d

An alternative approach is to create a walking bassline riff that spells out each chord in a progression. This works particularly well for a blues, of course, and is a sound heard on countless Rock 'n' Roll records. This rhythm part spells out a blues in E Major.

Example 2e

Lastly, Example 2f shows how you can begin to combine the walking bassline approach with chords to create a fuller sound (demonstrated over an A major chord). Play alternate up and downstrokes with your pick across the E, A and D strings, and keep the swinging rhythm going. There are lots of small variations you can make to this idea to keep things interesting, so do experiment with it.

Example 2f

The next few examples highlight some popular *offbeat* Rockabilly rhythms. The first of these is a style known as *skanking*. The rhythm tends to accent the two and four of the beat, and you'll most likely have heard this kind of idea played by Ska bands.

Skank Rhythm

In Example 2g, strum with a steady down-up, down-up 1/8 note pattern. The characteristic trait of this style is that beats one, two, three and four of every bar are played with a muted down stroke – the chord doesn't sound at all (indicated by an X in the Tab). Then, the upper notes of each chord shape sound on the offbeats.

If you count "1 **and** 2 **and** 3 **and** 4 **and**" for every bar, the "and" is the accented chord, played with an upstroke. Here's how it sounds:

Example 2g

Example 2h is another form of skanking, but with a more complicated rhythm. The rhythm jumps between 1/4 notes and 1/8 notes for effect. Although I've played an entire progression here for demonstration purposes, you may not want to use this kind of idea all the time. It works well when used sparingly, for effect.

Example 2h

Offbeat Swing Rhythm

Now we turn to the offbeat accented rhythm style you'll have heard on dozens of Elvis' recordings. Whereas some Rock 'n' Roll based rhythms are very rigid, Swing rhythm tends to be much freer and expressive. Again, it relies on accenting offbeats, but this time it's not done in a regimented fashion. In Swing, the bass player will often play a walking pattern, and this gives the guitarist more freedom to decide what should be highlighted by way of contrast.

Here's a swinging 12-bar blues rhythm part in G Major. The accents are mostly played on the offbeats with some small variations.

Example 2i

Example 2j is a rhythm part with further variation ideas for you. It shows how you can develop licks by spicing up chord voicings, sliding into chords, and varying the accents.

Example 2j

C13   G6

Eb9   D9

Travis Picking

Although it's highly unlikely that he invented this style of rhythm playing, Merle Travis was pivotal in pioneering this picking style that is essential to Country and Rockabilly music. Travis was born in 1917 and he adopted the picking style that was popular in his native state of Kentucky at that time. As is the way with folk music, songs and traditional techniques are passed down the generations, and previous noteworthy exponents were travelling coalman/musician Arnold Schultz, and Kennedy Jones who wrote one of the most famous pieces of music using this style: *Cannonball Rag*.

The essence of Travis picking is the alternating bass note and chord pattern. Bass notes are accentuated on beats one and three of each bar, and chords or melodic fills fit in between. When Tommy Emmanuel teaches this style he aptly calls it the *Boom Chick* approach.

If you listen to Tommy or Chet Atkins play, you'll hear that their Travis picking is fairly reserved compared to Rockabilly. Rockabilly took the idea and turned it up to 10! In this music it's played with the characteristic cutting sound and plenty of attitude and attack.

Mastering the style

The most challenging aspect of this style is getting the thumb and fingers to work independently. I'll also throw a spanner in the works at this point and say that I use a hybrid approach for Travis picking – a combination of pick and fingers that is a departure from the original approach. Here's a quick comparison of the traditional way of Travis picking and the way that I and other Rockabilly players do it. You can decide which method works best for you:

Traditional style: In traditional Travis picking, the thumb plays the low E, A, D and G strings, while the index and middle fingers look after the B and high E strings respectively. (In fact, Merle Travis only used his thumb and index finger in a *pinching* style).

Hybrid style: I grip the pick between by thumb and index finger and the pick plays the low E, A and D strings. This leaves the middle and ring fingers to pick out melodic lines and pluck the high notes of chords on the G, B and high E strings. The ring finger jumps between the B and high E as required.

Hybrid style is perhaps more prevalent among Rockabilly players because the pick produces more volume and a harder attack. This helps to maintain the right tone, but if this method is new to you, it's fine to play with the traditional style. The pieces in this chapter can be played either way. Here are some guidelines to get you started (there is no audio for these exercises).

Step 1: first, train your thumb to play alternating bassline patterns. Using the standard open E chord below, try Exercise 1. Use *only* the thumb to play the notes (or the pick if you're hybrid picking). Make the notes that fall on beats one and three *louder* than beats two and four.

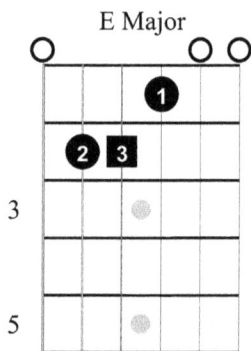

E Major

Exercise 1

Most of the time you'll want the bassline to be slightly muted, while the chords or melodic lines ring out, so this calls for some palm muting. Place the flesh of your picking hand gently on the bridge/saddle of the guitar, so the flesh is just in contact with the strings. You should be able to play the picking pattern and mute the strings at the same time. Try Exercise 2, which introduces a new chord, and palm mute the strings throughout.

Exercise 2

Step 2: next, introduce the fingers. When you can play a rock-solid alternating bass pattern, it's time to add some higher notes. If your coordination begins to falter, remember that the key is to train yourself to play the bass part first. Practice it until you can do it virtually unconsciously!

This is the part where you work on developing thumb/finger independence. The aim is to keep the bassline thudding away, using palm muting, while the upper notes of the chord ring out. Play Exercise 3 and adjust your technique until you can allow the high notes to keep ringing while the bass accompanies underneath.

Exercise 3

This has been a crash course on Travis picking! Space won't allow me to fully do it justice here, but you now understand the basic principle of it – everything else is embellishment. For a comprehensive guide, do check out Levi Clay's excellent book *The Country Fingerstyle Guitar Method* which covers this topic in detail and will help you to perfect your technique.

Now onto the licks…

Here is a relatively simple example to begin with, based around an open C major chord. The bass alternates between C and G notes. In the higher register I accent a D note on the B string, third fret. This changes the basic open C major chord to a Cadd9. Listen to the audio to capture the right feel.

Example 2k

Example 2l is slightly more involved and requires you to pluck more notes in the high register. It's based around a C major chord played in eighth position. If you're playing fingerstyle, then the thumb takes care of the low E, A, D and G strings, and the index and middle finger are assigned to the B and high E strings respectively.

If you're playing hybrid style like me, in this example the pick covers the E, A and D strings, and the middle finger looks after the G string. The ring finger's job is to jump between the B and high E strings as required. To play Example 2l, I also hook my thumb over the neck to play the low C bass note.

Example 2l

Here's a similar lick to the previous one, but with different ornamentation on the high strings.

Example 2m

Here's a more challenging piece to get your teeth into during practice sessions. If it looks/sounds a bit intimidating at first, the key is to slow things right down and work on small sections until you've locked the mechanics of the picking hand into muscle memory. Once the chord grips and picking technique are in place, play along to a slow-medium metronome and don't speed up until you can play it cleanly.

Example 2n

Here's a full blues progression in C Major. This example shows how you might combine Travis picking with banjo rolls (in bars 6, 9 and 10). If the banjo rolls are a bit of a curve ball, we're going to focus on them in detail in Chapter Four! Once again, slow things right down and work on smaller sections before attempting the whole thing.

Example 2o

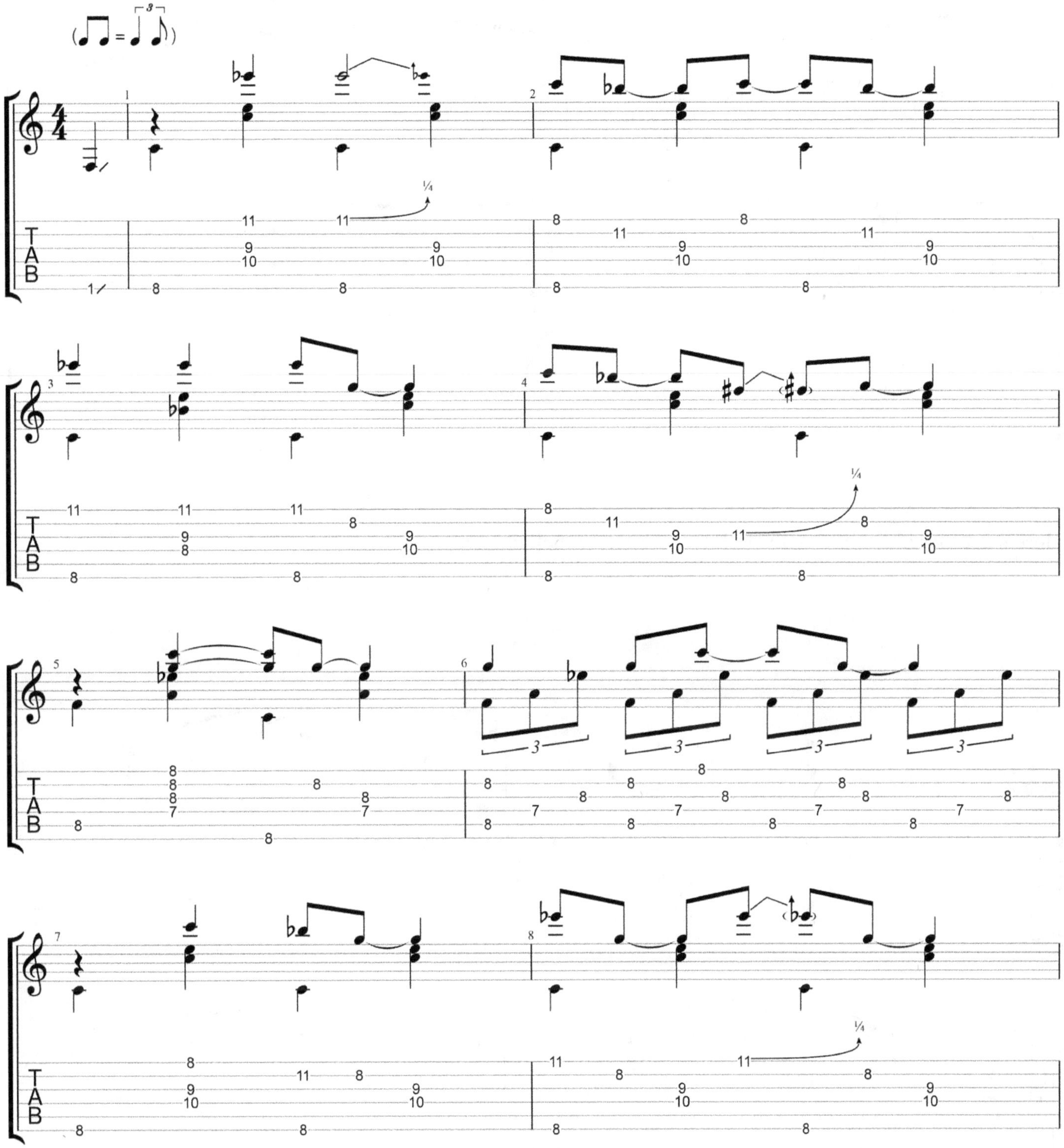

Here's another blues in C with slightly different embellishments.

Example 2p

The next example switches to the key of E Major and demonstrates a nice way of embellishing an open E7 chord.

Example 2q

If the previous example was the opening bars of a blues in E Major, here is how I might play over the IV chord (A7).

Example 2r

And here's how I might approach the V chord (B7) and the transition back to the E7.

Example 2s

The next example returns to the key of C Major for a gentler example of how you might Travis pick to accompany a singer. It's played with less attack, but there is still plenty of movement to provide a full accompaniment.

Example 2t

Finally, no examination of Travis picking would be complete without a nod to one of its originators, Kennedy Jones. Here's a practice piece in the style of *Cannonball Rag*. Look out for the pull-off run down to the G bass note at the end.

Example 2u

We've covered the essential rhythms of Rockabilly. It will take time to perfect your Travis picking, so do persevere with it. For a while it may feel as though you need two brains, but eventually it will just click for you! In the next chapter, we move on to look at a collection of licks inspired by the styles of some Rockabilly greats.

Chapter Three – Rockabilly Heroes

It was important to address the rhythm guitar ideas we looked at in the previous chapter, because rhythm is such a big part of Rockabilly style, but from here on in, it's all about the licks!

At the beginning of this book, I mentioned some of the great Rockabilly guitar players who have inspired me over the years. In this chapter, you'll learn a collection of licks that give a nod to the style of these greats and a couple of other noteworthy players. So many other great names could have been included here, but there is only so much space, so it was necessary to be selective.

Eddie Cochran

We'll begin with some Eddie Cochran licks. Example 3a captures the hard hitting aggressive edge of Eddie's playing. Why play something complicated when you can grab people's attention with a dramatic riff-based solo? Dig in for this one.

Example 3a

Despite his aggressive edge, Eddie was a fine guitar player who could play articulate lines when the music called for it. Here's a double-stop lick with a repeating motif played over an A chord.

Example 3b

The next lick continues this idea over a D7 chord.

Example 3c

Now here's a different A major chord riff. When faced with several bars of one chord, double-stops like these break the monotony of just chugging on one chord.

Example 3d

Finally, here's a full 12-bar – Eddie style. It begins the same way as Example 3a, but then heads in a different direction. Play this example with consistent 1/8 note downstrokes all the way through.

Example 3e

Scotty Moore

Scotty used a big Gibson L5 for most of his Elvis recordings and invented lots of licks that are now standard Rockabilly vocabulary. His ideas always had a strong rhythmic element to them. Scotty was a versatile player, but here we are focusing on some of his double-stop ideas. In this first lick, notice how effective it can be to slide into double-stops from a half-step below.

Example 3f

Here is a swinging double-stop lick that works well over a shuffle groove.

Example 3g

Lastly, this double-stop lick incorporates a bend, played over a D major chord.

Example 3h

Cliff Gallup

Cliff Gallup had more Jazz and Country influence in his playing than some of the other guitar players mentioned here and played some thoughtful lines alongside the standard Rock 'n' Roll vocabulary. Here's an example of the type of thing he might play.

Example 3i

Cliff's melodic lines always had a great sense of time and swing. Here's a neat lick you can play over an A major chord.

Example 3j

Here's a typical Cliff-type lick that uses the hybrid major/minor pentatonic scale in position three played over a G7 chord. The line weaves around the chord tones and includes some chromatic passing notes.

Example 3k

Here's a lick you can play over the transition from the IV chord (C major in this instance) to the I chord (G major) in a blues. This lick is all about the rhythm, so aim to play it with plenty of bounce.

Example 3l

Here's another G major bouncing lick, this time based around position seven.

Example 3m

Example 3m has a simple repeating phrase and is played over a G major chord.

Example 3n

The final Cliff example is played over the transition from the V chord (D7) to the I chord (G major) in a G blues. The main idea in bars 1-2 is that the notes on the B string descend chromatically from a D note (B string, fret fifteen), similar to a pedal tone.

Example 3o

Joe Maphis

Joe Maphis' recording career began when he was "discovered" by Merle Travis. He played on countless Rockabilly sessions in the 1950s but notably played lead on many of the Ricky Nelson sessions, prior to James Burton becoming Ricky's permanent guitarist. He was also a regular performer on the *Town Hall Party* TV show, where he often played a variety of instruments including fiddle, double bass and banjo.

Joe was an incredibly gifted guitar player, who also had a flair for the dramatic. Example 3o is the kind of "effect" lick he would often play.

Example 3p

Joe had amazing technique, so could play fast, fluid lines with ease. Here's a Joe-style lick over a C major chord.

Example 3q

Example 3q is a simple lick that highlights the Country flavour in Joe's playing.

Example 3r

Example 3r is a similar idea, but shows how a line like this can be embellished differently with a few variations.

Example 3s

The final idea is played over an E major chord and highlights Joe's fondness for Country style hammer-ons/pull-offs.

Example 3t

Grady Martin

As mentioned in the introduction, Grady Martin was a guitarist with the Nashville A-Team – the elite players of their day, who backed everyone from Elvis Presley and Patsy Cline, to Jim Reeves and Bob Dylan. As such he was a very versatile player who could turn his hand to a number of styles. He also developed the discipline of a studio musician to be able to come up with well-conceived guitar parts at the drop of a hat.

To begin with, here's a neat double-stop idea with a repeating rhythm that can be played over an E major chord.

Example 3u

Here's a short lick played over a D major chord. The idea here is to bend the note on the G string, tenth fret a half step, while simultaneously picking the B string, seventh fret. The half step bend means that both notes will be a D, but with a different tone, which produces a pleasing "out of phase" sound.

Example 3v

Here's a typical example of how Grady might construct a song intro. It begins with an A minor chord, then moves into a memorable lick that repeats with a variation. This kind of lick is ideal as the beginning or ending to a song.

Example 3w

Albert Lee

The mention of Albert Lee's name here might surprise some, but for years he has been a great exponent of Country rock and many of his licks and ideas have been "repurposed" and found their way into common Rockabilly vocabulary. So here are some nice Albert-style double-stop ideas you can add into your solos.

First, here is a way of playing a C blues progression using double-stops. In the audio example I play this at an easily manageable speed, but Albert might play something like this at least twice as fast!

Example 3x

The next example is a driving lick over an A major chord. The double-stops are fragments of the A chord descending the neck.

Example 3y

Here's a continuation of this idea, but this time I've added a concluding chord. Licks like this are a useful way to end a solo or finish a song.

Example 3z

Played over a D major chord, this lick has a strong Country flavour and is the kind of line you can play as the intro to a ballad or slower tempo tune.

Example 3z1

Brian Setzer

Any list of trailblazing Rockabilly guitar players must surely include Brian Setzer. While many guitarists were trying hard to recreate the authentic sound and style of the classic Rockabilly of years past, Setzer showed a glorious disregard for that pursuit. He loved the music, of course, but put his own unique spin on it, incorporating an American rock sensibility. His style is so unique that it encouraged me to try and find my own, and I'm very thankful for his influence. He's known for his ability to play flashier, dynamic licks, so here are a few Setzer-like ideas for you.

Here's a looping idea over a G major chord with a 1/4 bend, otherwise known as a blues *curl*. You're not trying to play a different note with the bend, you're just pushing it very slightly sharp.

Example 3z2

This idea works over a D major chord. A characteristic of Setzer's style is to not just bend notes, but bend double-stops too. The double-stop at the end of bar one is pushed slightly out of tune with another blues curl.

Example 3z3

Here's another lick based around the G major chord in position three. The opening double-stop is followed by a bluesy lick with more curls.

Example 3z4

This example in A major begins with a pick-up phrase that is played with a fast rake from the G to high E strings. Play the rake with a single continuous downstroke and "push through" the strings.

Example 3z5

Now let's explore the jazzier side of Brian's playing. Played over a G major chord, this lick could easily have been played by electric jazz guitar pioneer Charlie Christian.

Example 3z6

The next example features a repeating idea in bars 3-4 that emphasises the major third of the underlying G major chord.

Example 3z7

To end, here's a more aggressive idea that begins with a riff which turns into a lick. The riff section suggests an underlying C minor chord, but then the lick shifts into C major. It's the class Blues minor/major switch used by so many of the blues/rock greats.

Example 3z8

In this chapter we've looked at the styles of the Rockabilly players who've influenced me the most. Hopefully you can see how this melting pot of styles contains a wealth of ideas to explore. As you develop your skills, it's really important to take hold of the ideas you like and transpose them to other keys. This will help you to absorb them into your playing, so they become a permanent part of your musical vocabulary. Also, do as much listening as you can. Don't forget the Spotify playlist that comes with this book, which you can use to explore more of the music of each featured artist.

In this next chapter, we take things up a gear to focus on some of the trickier licks that form a part of this style.

Chapter Four – Advanced Techniques

A feature of Rockabilly guitar playing that shows its strong Country roots is the use of hammer-on/pull-off licks and the classic "banjo roll". In this chapter you'll learn some licks for each of these techniques, and to finish we'll play some licks that combine the two.

Hammer-ons and Pull-offs

To begin with, here's a well-known pull-off lick based around an open E chord. It's a classic, so it's good to have this one in your repertoire. It also sounds great because the open strings continue to ring as you change position.

This is a good lick to practice your pull-off technique. It's easy to be lazy with pull-offs and not execute them cleanly. In bar one, fret the first note of the triplet (G on the high E string, third fret) with your middle finger and pick downwards. Then quickly hammer-on to fret two with your index finger to sound the second note. Pull off with your index finger (moving it away from the string, down towards the floor) to sound the open string. Only the first note of the triplet is picked, but if you follow the technique you should get a nice even sound with each note the same volume.

Example 4a

Here's a tricker lick based around a position three G chord. It uses the notes of the combined major/minor pentatonic shape. You'll need to use your pinky finger to execute the hammer-on to the high E string, sixth fret, while your index finger plays to G note at the third fret. It's a good lick for strengthening that pinky!

Example 4b

Example 4c uses the same scale as the previous example and fits nicely over the G7 chord at the start of a G blues (although this lick will fit over any chord in a G blues). This time it's a sequenced lick that loops in a two-bar pattern. In bar four, I end the lick by playing the top notes of a G chord, but you could continue to loop it for as long as you want, repeating bars 1-2.

Example 4c

The final hammer-on/pull-off lick is another sequencing idea. Played over an E major chord, this is an attention-grabbing lick, because it uses very wide intervals against the open high E and B strings. Once again, your focus should be on getting this sounding clean and even.

Example 4d

Banjo Roll Technique

Now we move onto another classic Rockabilly technique. As the name suggests, the banjo roll was borrowed from classic banjo technique and repurposed for guitar. A banjo roll is an arpeggio, played as a triplet, using a hybrid picking technique.

Typically in Rockabilly banjo rolls, a triplet is played over every beat in a bar of 4/4 (count 123, 123, 123, 123). Sometimes you'll hear guitar players like Tommy Emmanuel do double-time rolls (sextuplets rather than triplets – six notes for every beat in a bar of 4/4), but here we are only tackling the triplet variety!

Exercise 1 is based around an open E major chord and will help you acquaint yourself with the technique if it's new to you. It's all about the picking hand and there are two ways to play this.

Method 1: If you're an experienced traditional fingerpicker, this method might feel most natural to you. Strike the note on the G string, first fret with your thumb, then pluck the open B string with the index finger, and the open high E string with the middle finger.

Method 2: Alternatively, you can play it like me. I use a pick and fingers hybrid method. With the pick gripped between thumb and index finger, I play the first two notes of the roll with the pick, picking downwards through the strings, then play the third note with the middle finger.

Using whichever picking approach suits you best, practice the roll slowly to begin with to lock the picking pattern into muscle memory. Aim to get all the notes sounding as loudly as each other. A common mistake with this technique is to introduce a brief "lag" after hitting the first note with the thumb or pick, before the next note sounds. Even a small lag can result in an uneven note spacing, which upsets the rhythm. Play with a metronome and count "123, 123" out loud as you play to iron out any lag.

Exercise 1 (no audio)

Most of the examples here are known as *forward rolls*, which simply means they are picked downwards, beginning with the thumb. Here's the first. In the audio example you'll hear me start slowly then speed up, so you can hear what I'm doing more clearly. This lick is based around an F9 chord in eighth position. Hold down this chord shape throughout.

This lick also introduces a string skip. The last note of each triplet alternates between notes on the G and B strings. It's a good lick to test how robust your technique is. The challenge is to play it cleanly and still make the note divisions sound even.

Example 4e

Here's a banjo roll style lick you can play over a G7 chord. It requires a little bit of a stretch for the fretting hand, but sounds really effective. To play this, barre your fretting hand index finger over the high E and B strings at the third fret and keep them in place to act as an anchor. The notes on the G string are played with the pinky.

Example 4f

Ideas like Example 4f are moveable. Here's a similar idea, shifted up a tone and based around an A major chord. This example shows how I'd incorporate this idea as part of a lick over the first four bars of a blues in A Major.

Example 4g

The next example uses a *reverse roll* rather than a *forward roll*. This just means that you pick in the *opposite* direction to the licks you've played so far – from high strings to low.

This lick also features a nice little trick you can use during a G blues. When it comes to the IV chord (C7), you can use this moveable diminished 7th chord shape to spice things up.

E°

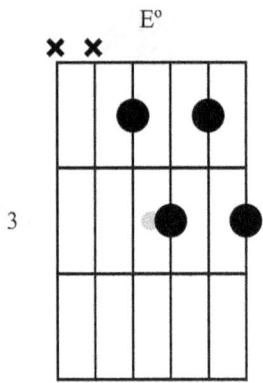

This is the type of idea that crops up in Brian Setzer's playing. It's common to use a diminished 7th chord as a substitute for a dominant 7th. Like most chord substitution ideas, it works on the basis of common notes.

The E° chord above uses the notes: E, G, Bb, C#

The C7 chord is built using the notes C, E, G, Bb

They share three notes in common. The E° chord contains the 3rd (E), 5th (G) and 7th (Bb) intervals of C7, so it strongly describes the C7 sound.

These small diminished shapes are also moveable, and you can shift them around the neck in minor third intervals (a distance of three frets). When you move the shape, the "new" chord is just an *inversion* of the original chord (it has all the same notes, just in a different order). Example 4h moves from Edim7 to Gdim7 to Bbdim7 to C#dim7, but they are all inversions of the same chord and all describe the C7 sound.

Example 4h

Here's a different flavoured banjo roll lick for you, played over an A minor chord. It's not your obvious banjo roll idea, but I played it using the technique. Banjo roll picking technique is great to execute licks that skip back and forth between strings.

Example 4i

To end this section, here's a complete banjo roll blues in E major. It combines a couple of the ideas we've seen so far and rolls its way throughout the entire progression. This is reminiscent of a solo Eddie Cochran played, but it was a studio outtake, so you can't actually listen to a recording of it. I suggest slowing this one right down and getting familiar with the fretting hand movements first. Then focus on getting your picking hand rolling smooth and even. When it's played up to tempo, the effect is impressive.

Example 4j – Banjo Roll Blues

Combining Techniques

To end this chapter, I've put together some licks that combine the techniques we've discussed, and weave together single-note phrases with hammer-ons/pull-offs and banjo rolls.

To begin with, here is a longer line in the key of E Major that begins with a simple pentatonic phrase before moving into a banjo roll in bars 3-4. In bars 5-6, you'll find a hammer-on/pull-off idea similar to Example 4a. The difference here is that the notes on the high E and B strings are played simultaneously – so it's kind of a double-stop pull-off!

In the very last bar, be sure to attack your whammy bar if you have one! Hit the low E string, then plunge the whammy bar and control it so that it comes smoothly back to pitch.

Example 4k

Example 4l is a full 12-bar blues progression in G Major. Bars 13-14 here are an ending that I've tagged on. Bars 3-4 feature the kind of pull-off lick we've seen already, and bars 5-6 outline the chords with double-stops.

The lick in bars 7-8 is executed with banjo roll technique. Slow these bars down and make sure your technique is squeaky clean here, because you also need to make a 1/4 bend with your pinky.

Example 4l

Here's another example of combining techniques. The banjo roll in bars 3-4 (over a G chord) is followed by a Travis picked phrase in bar five (over a D chord), before returning to the banjo roll idea in bar six.

Example 4m

Example 4n is another 12-bar blues sequence, this time in A Major. Here we begin with a double-stop pedal tone idea (i.e. one note repeats while the notes around it change). We move into a fast reverse banjo rolled passage in bars 5-6, followed by forward banjo rolls in bars 7-8, and reverse rolls again in bars 9-10. We finish with some minor pentatonic double stops and a run down the blues scale in the final two bars.

Example 4n

To end this chapter, here's another double-stop lick that works over A major, with a fast ascending run that spans bars 3-4. Use hammer-ons for the fast run.

Example 4o

Chapter Five – Rockabilly Solos

To complete the book, I wanted to give you some longer examples that illustrate how to construct a Rockabilly-style solo. Because most often a Rockabilly band will comprise only guitar, bass and drums, you'll notice that the solos here have one thing in common: they are full-sounding arrangements and there isn't too much single-line soloing.

In Rockabilly, it's less common to have continuous walking basslines than it is in Jazz, and this can leave a "hole" in the sound if the guitarist is playing lots of single-line solos. It helps to create a fuller sound if the guitar solo includes double-stops, chord passages and riff-like phrases. Here are a dozen solo ideas for you in a variety of styles.

Example 5a is a hard hitting chord-based solo over two choruses of an E Major blues. In bar five, I play the A9/C# chord by playing the C# note (A string, fourth fret) with the pinky finger, while the index finger holds down the E note (D string, second fret).

In bars 21-22, the C7 and B7#9 chords are both voiced with the 5th interval in the bass (creating the sound of C7 over a G bass, and B7#9 over an F# bass). The effect of this is to create a bassline chromatic run down to the final E chord.

Example 5a

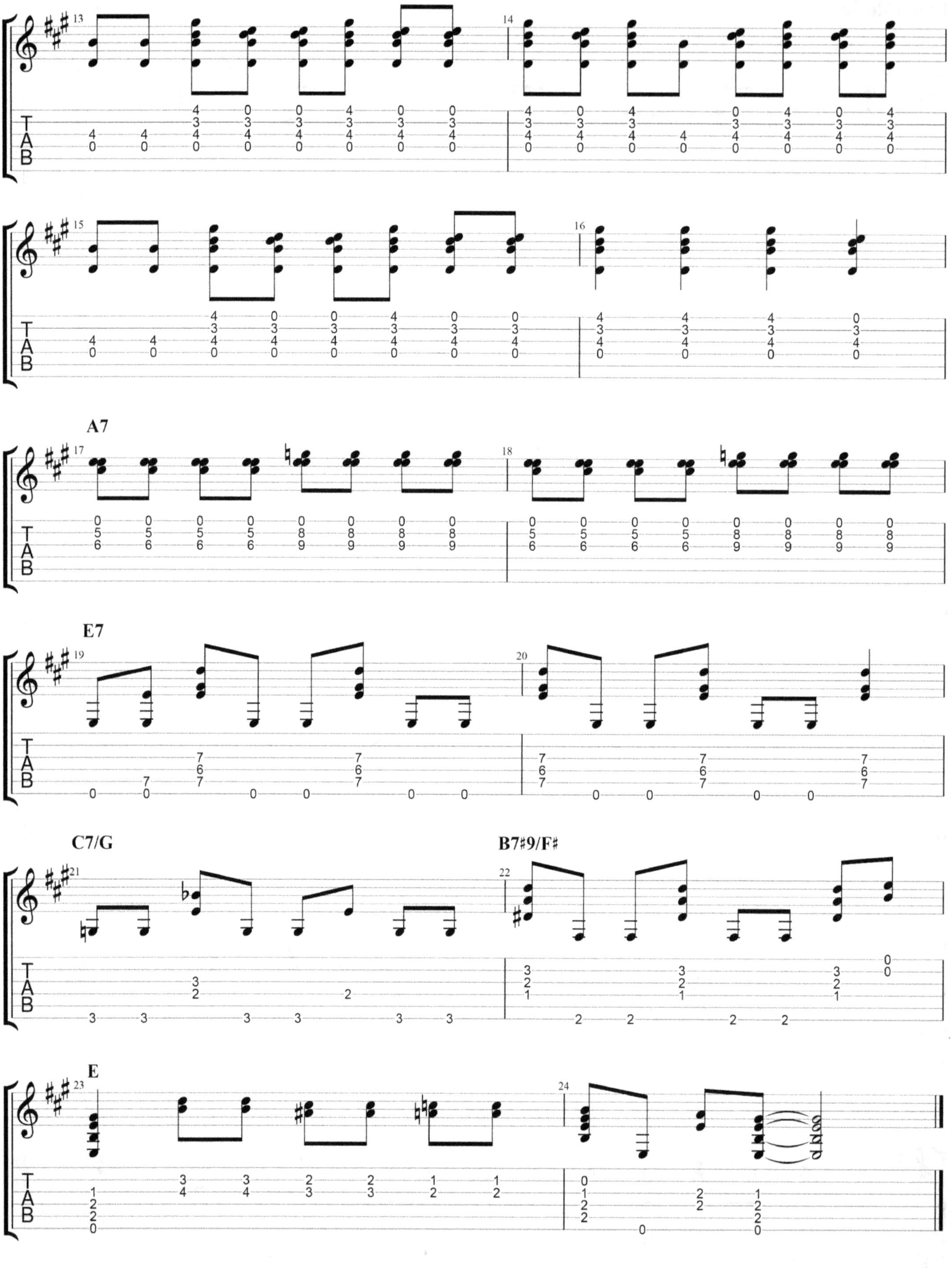
A7
E7
C7/G
B7♯9/F♯
E

If the arrangement of a song means that there's only room for a quick solo, or you are playing over the middle eight, then you may as well go for the jugular! Here's an eight-bar break in E major. Hit those double-stops at the twelfth fret hard and really make them sing out.

Example 5b

Example 5c is a 12-bar in E Major. As the main harmonic instrument in Rockabilly, lots of the tunes are written in guitar-friendly keys, which means you'll often be able to include open strings for a drone-like effect. Example 5c makes as much use as possible of this technique.

Example 5c

This next example is another take on an E blues, this time using more bends and double-stops. Sliding into chords helps to keep up the momentum in this solo.

Example 5d

Example 5e is two choruses of a blues in A Major. This is a solo that begins simply, but throws in more complex ideas as it builds. The first chorus features a pretty standard chord-based riff. In bars 13-16 I play a pedal tone idea, keeping the high A note (high E string, fifth fret) going while notes descend against it on the B string. Bars 17-22 feature some Country-influenced licks.

Look out for the banjo-rolled lick in bars 19-20. This is a nice descending idea that produces a cascading effect and lands on the open A string. The solo ends with a standard Rock 'n' Roll lick.

Example 5e

If you find yourself playing in a Rockabilly setup that has a singer strumming on acoustic guitar, then of course, there is more scope to play single line solos. Equally, you can just depend on creating an absolutely massive guitar tone with lots of slap-back echo and a touch of overdrive, like Brian Setzer. This solo is played over a blues in G Major.

Example 5f

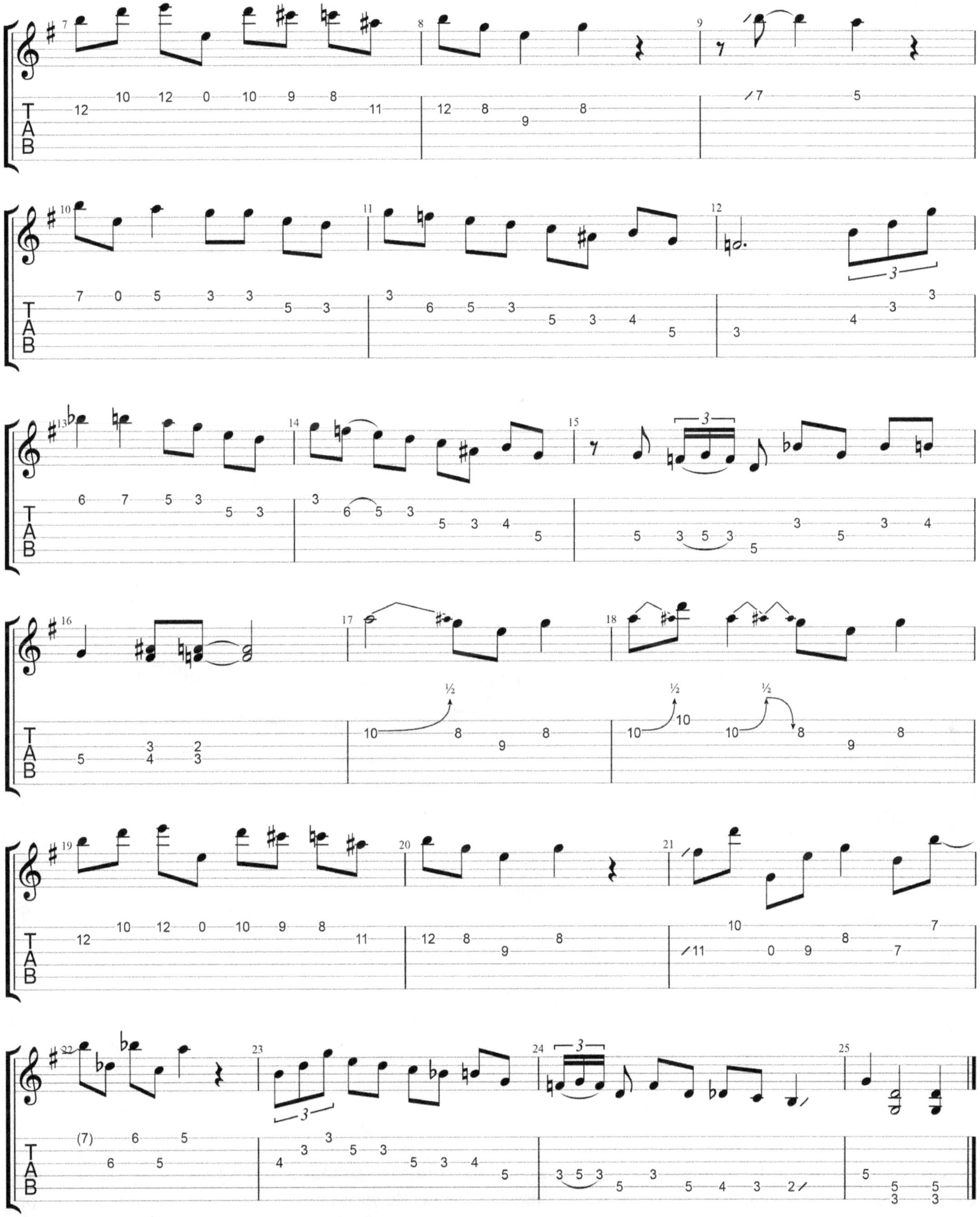

Here is another pass at a blues in G Major. This solo begins with single-note lines, then switches to Travis picking when the IV chord (C9) comes in. We return to single-note phrases from bar seven to the end. Look out for the fast pull-offs to open strings in the last two bars.

Example 5g

Now for something a little different. Here's a slower tempo, old-time sounding blues in E Major that is almost exclusively Travis picked, apart from the occasional banjo roll. Be sure to use some palm muting for this one to capture the same feel as the audio.

Example 5h

Example 5i is another Travis picked solo over a G Major blues. This one is executed more in the style of Cliff Gallup. As before, if you find any of the passages tricky, slow things right down and focus on nailing smaller sections at a time.

Example 5i

Next, we have an A Major blues. This solo is part line and part riff. A great way to construct a memorable solo is to play a simple riff and punctuate it with single lines. It gives your audience something solid to hang onto.

Example 5j

Here's an alternative take on the A blues. I mix things up here, with a banjo rolled section and some Country-style double-stops.

Example 5k

This last example is a piece I wrote called *Darrel's Boogie*, based around a blues in E Major. The first three bars here set up the tempo and the 12-bar progression begins proper at bar four (indicated by the double bar line). This is a fun challenge for you to work on during your practice times. It's all about keeping the bassline going and seeing what you can fit around it. Have fun with it and try to come up with your own ideas for embellishment.

Example 5l

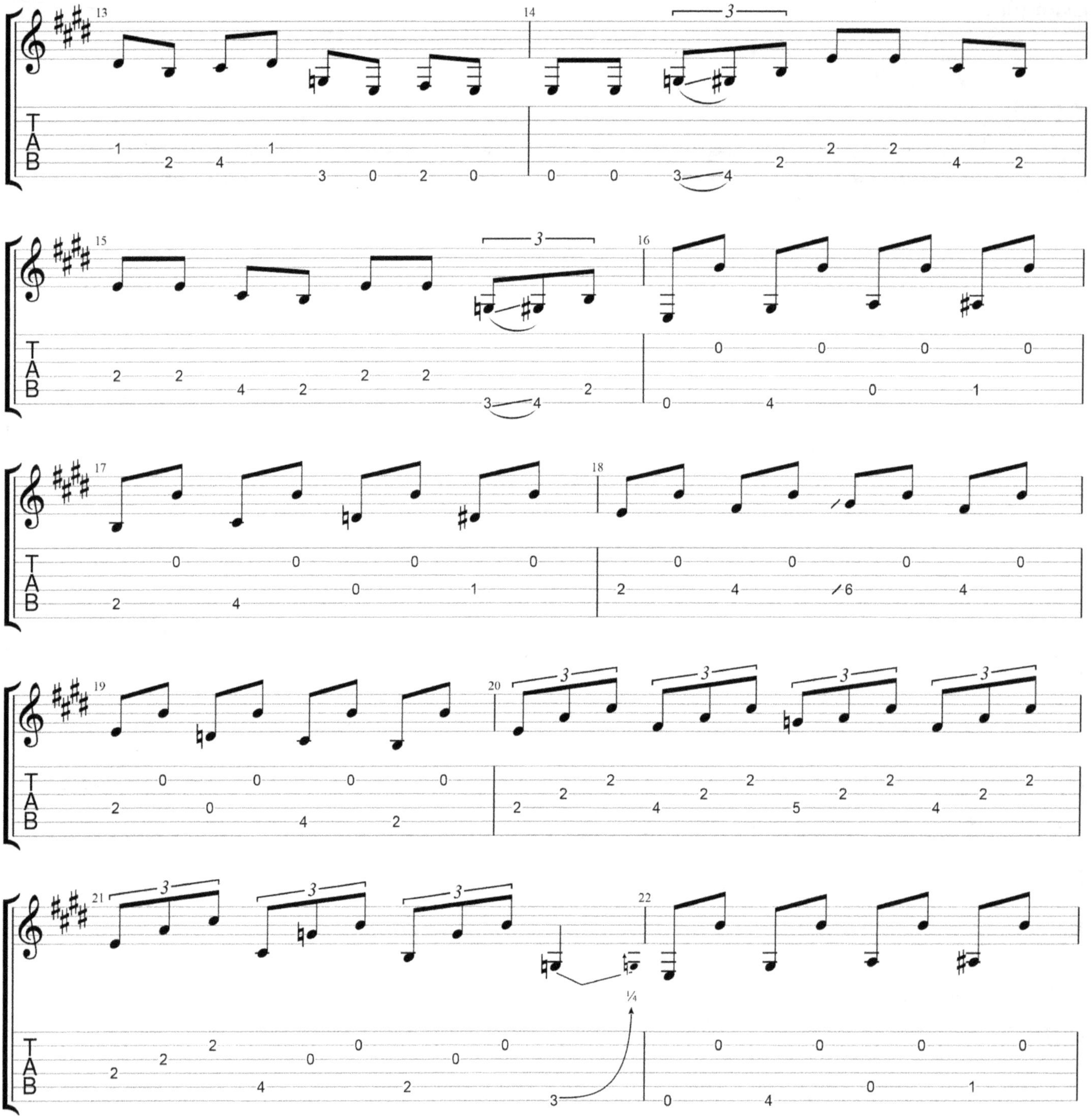
13
14
15
16
17
18
19
20
21
22
TAB
¼

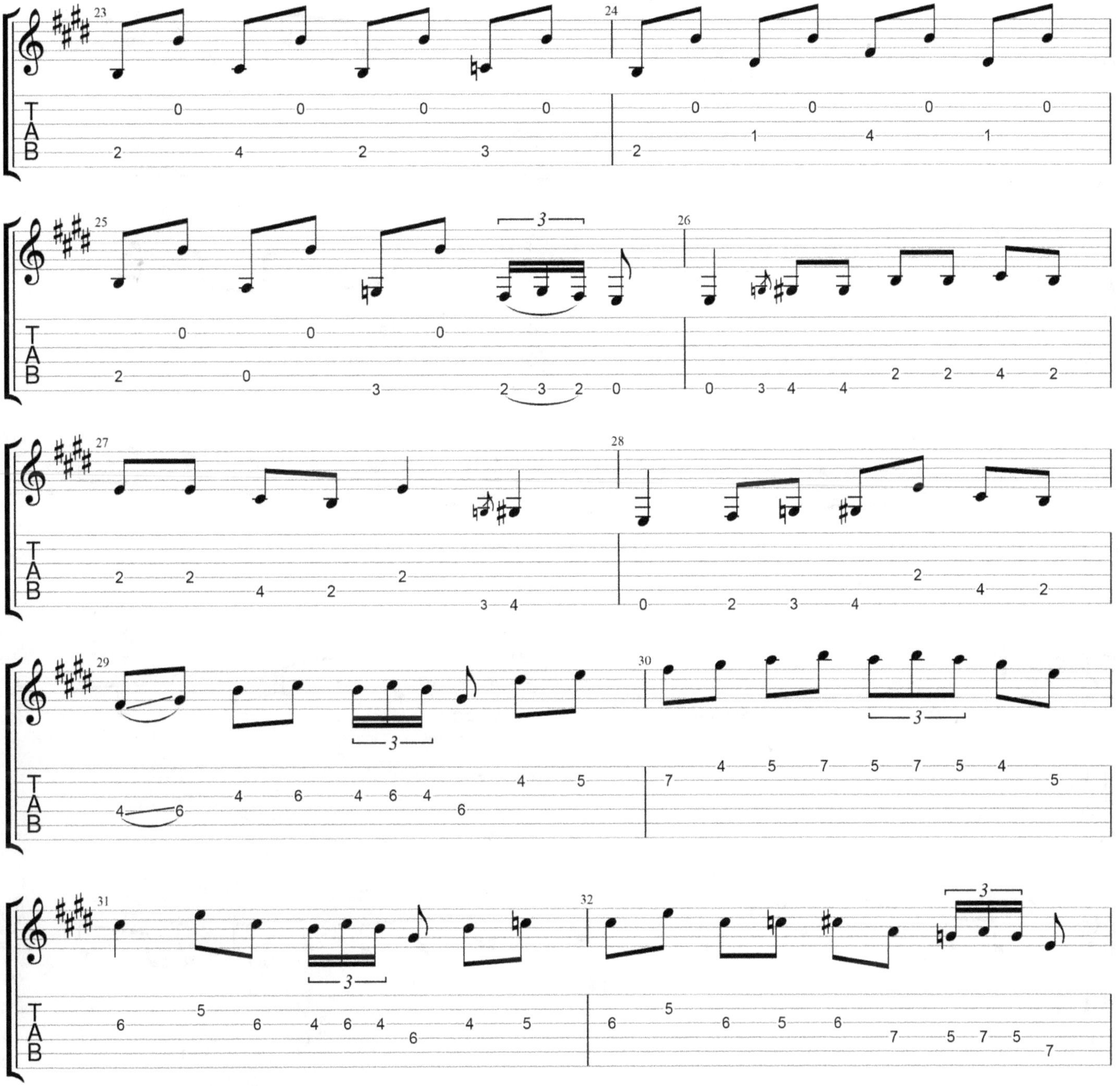

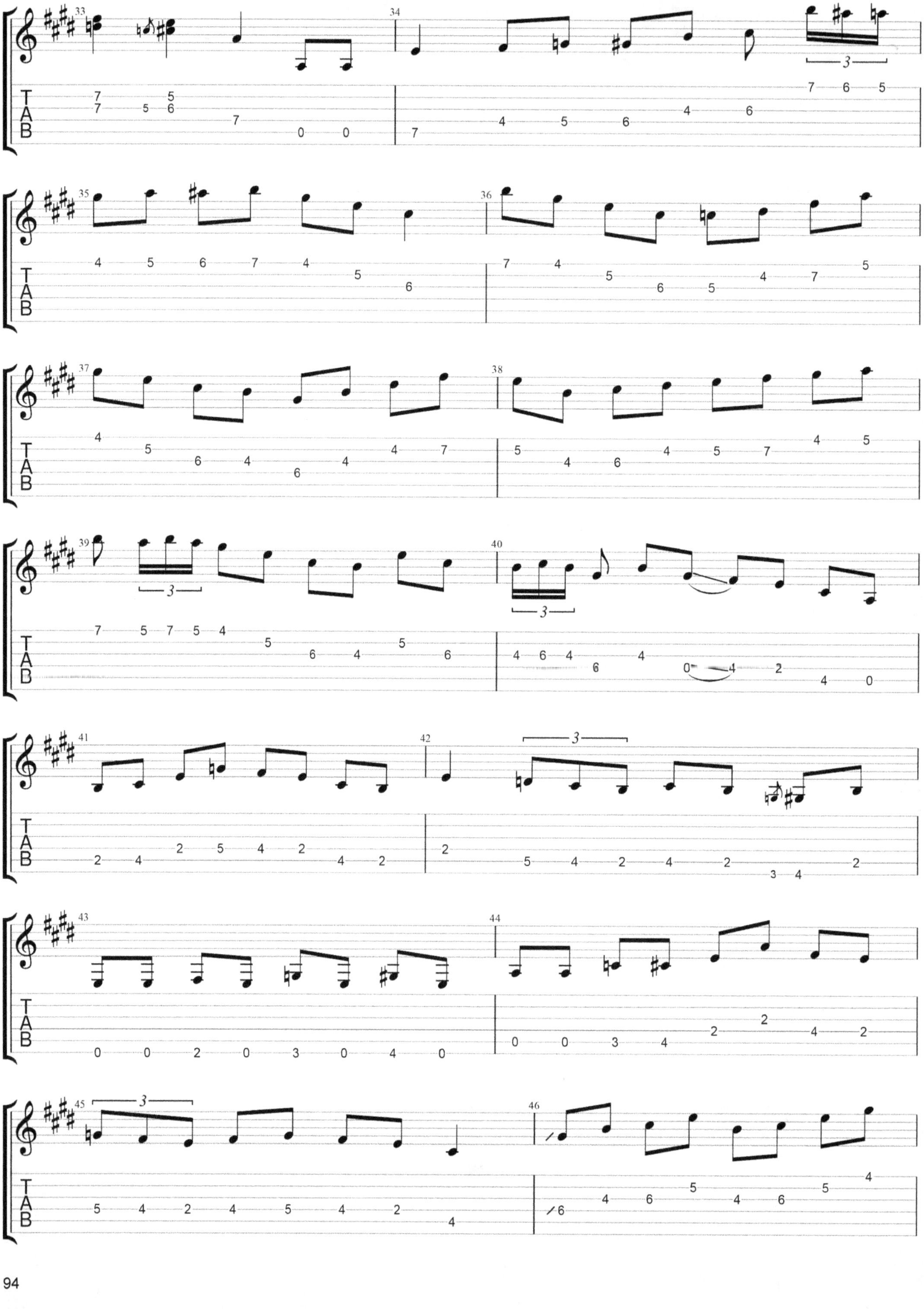

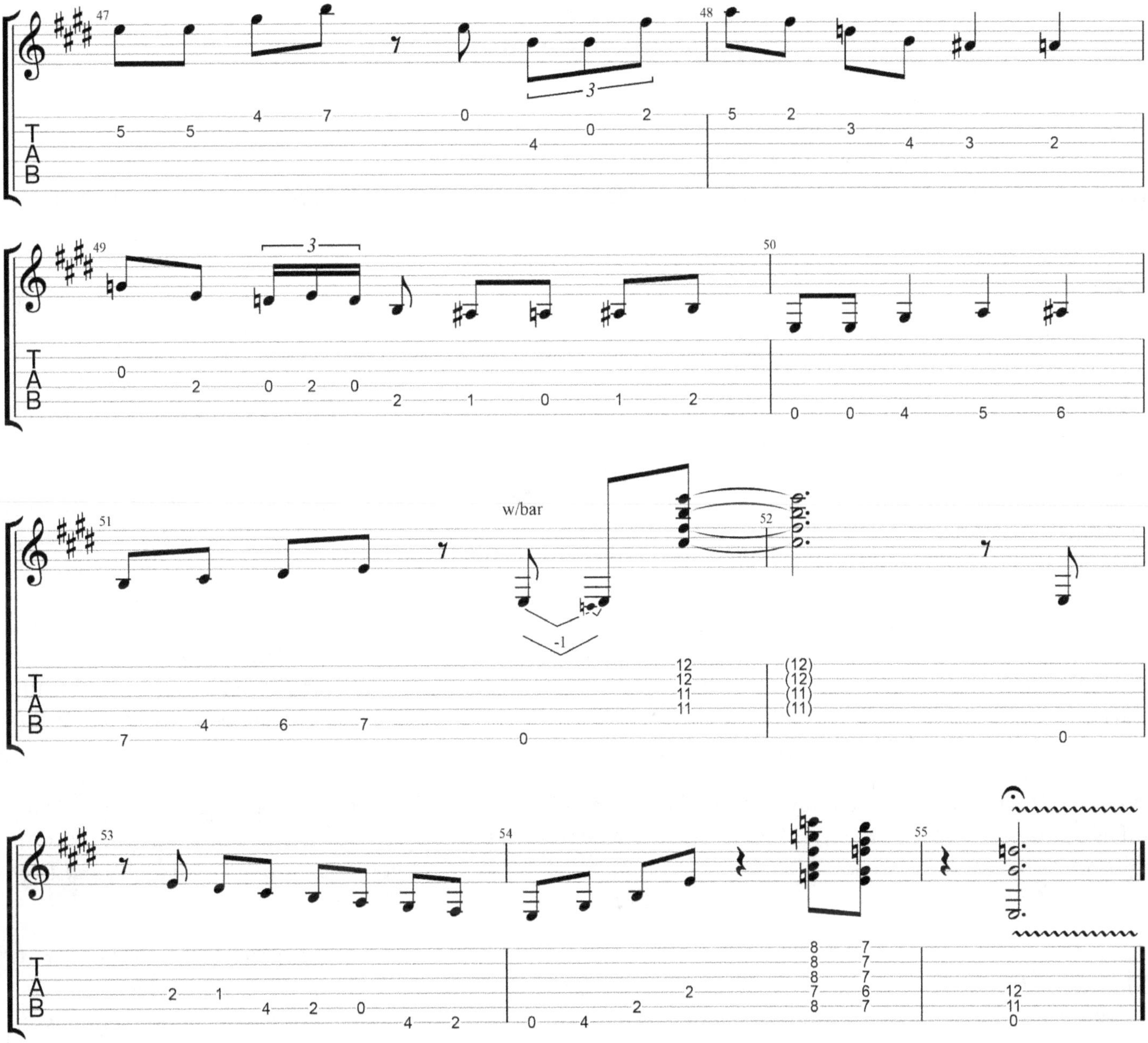
w/bar
-1

Guitars, Amps & Effects

When it comes to my typical onstage set-up, I've always preferred to use new amps, guitars and effects as opposed to vintage equipment. That might surprise a few people, but if you're gigging as much as I tend to, reliability is essential. I've never owned a vintage guitar or amp for the sole purpose of using them on gigs.

Guitars

My first Gretsch was made in 1989 and I purchased it brand new. It was the 40th guitar made by the newly resurrected Gretsch Company and one of the first to be imported into the UK. I used that on every gig and recording session until it was stolen from a theatre in Melton Mowbray in 1998. I also bought one of the first Fender Bassman '59 reissue amps that came out in the early 1990s and used that as my main amp for many years until it blew up! Unfortunately, it now gets used as a doorstop at Embassy Studios. As you can see, I've always bought new equipment that has a "vintage" look. That has always been more important to me than anything else. Nowadays, there is so much choice on the market that I thought it would be helpful to go over what I use.

I'm endorsed by Gretsch, so I use their guitars exclusively, but I would use them even if I wasn't, because to me they are the perfect guitars for Rockabilly. Thanks to Eddie Cochran, Cliff Gallup, Duane Eddy, Chet Atkins (yes, he played on many Rockabilly songs in the 1950s!) and many others from the golden era of this music, Gretsch defined the sound that I wanted to achieve. Let's not forget when Brian Setzer came along with the Stray Cats in the early 1980s, because he also made a huge impact on me.

As an aside, it's important to know that Rockabilly music wasn't just played on Gretsch guitars, so there are other options to explore. Scotty Moore was a Gibson man and his early work with Elvis was played on a Gibson 295. He later switched to the legendary L5, which he used for iconic recordings such as *Hound Dog, My Baby Left Me, Don't Be Cruel, Lawdy Miss Clawdy, King Creole* and more.

James Burton used a Telecaster. Joe Maphis used a twin-neck Mosrite guitar (check it out on YouTube). Grady Martin used a variety of guitars, but seemed to favour a Bigsby. (The Bigsby tremolo arm is legendary, but Bigsby made guitars too – some of them were pretty exotic looking!) Hank Garland also used Gibsons, as well as a variety of guitars for his numerous sessions in Nashville. Buddy Holly was famous for playing a Stratocaster, and on his early Rockabilly recordings in Nashville in 1956, Sonny Curtis used Buddy's guitar to play lead on songs such as *Rock Around With Ollie Vee, Love Me, Midnight Shift, Changing All Those Changes* and *Don't Come Back Knockin'*.

If the Gretsch is your thing, however, these days there are some great options available that won't break the bank. They all look the part and sound wonderful, so the choice is incredible. I heartily recommend the budget Electromatic series if you're thinking seriously of getting a Rockabilly axe but don't want to spend a fortune. The Gretsch 5120 is worthy of a look and strum if you see one in your local guitar shop.

I own seven Gretsch guitars. I have a Custom Shop 6120 that was built in 2008 by Stephen Stern – the legendary Gretsch Master Builder. It's a replica of the mid-50's 6120 and gets used mainly for recording and is rarely gigged. Stephen also made my 5170 (my main gigging guitar) which is a cross between a 6120 and a White Falcon. It has the neck dimensions and finish of a mid-50's 6120 but the body size and headstock of a Falcon.

I have a modern Duo Jet with Dynasonic pickups and a fixed-arm Bigsby that gets used for any gigs that require a Cliff Gallup sound. In fact, all my Gretsch guitars have a fixed-arm Bigsby, which means the arm does not sway or move away from you, as it's fixed in position just above the pick guard. The very first Bigsby tremolo units were all made like this and it is this model that was on Eddie Cochran's 6120. He never felt the need to change his, and if it was good enough for Eddie then it's good enough for me! They are not especially popular on modern guitars and, in fact, were not that popular back in the mid-50's, so Bigsby changed to the more familiar "sway" arm around 1956/57. Another influence from Eddie is the use of a Dynasonic (or DeArmond, as they were known back in the 1950's) pickup on the neck and a Gibson P90 on the bridge. I have that pick-up configuration on all my guitars except for the aforementioned Duo Jet. Over the years I've used original and reissue Dynasonics and I like the Seymour Duncan and TV Jones versions of both.

Other Gretsch guitars I own include a White Falcon, a Rancher acoustic, a six-string baritone, and an Eddie Cochran signature model 6120 that I take with me on gigs abroad.

Amps

I've also been lucky enough to be endorsed by Peavey for many years. After my Fender Bassman blew up, I bought a Peavey Delta Blues and I've never looked back. I've always had the 1x15" speaker as I feel it helps fatten up the Dynasonic pick-ups I use. This amp has never let me down. It's a real workhorse, always sounds great and is very robust. It's also very easy to instantly get the sound you want and that's incredibly important on gigs when you don't get a lot of time to set up. I always use the drive channel in order to get a slight amount of overdrive. I don't like too much distortion, just enough to take the edge off the clean sound. The amp is only 30 watts, but is plenty powerful for every gig I've ever done, be it at a pub or a huge festival.

Effects

As for effects, my personal belief has always been to keep things simple. When I first started gigging, I used whatever I could afford. There was not a great deal of choice as far as effects were concerned, as digital pedals were in their infancy, but I remember owning and gigging a very early Watkins Copicat echo. It was the blue and white box, which dates it to the very early 1960s. However, it was very noisy and went through tapes at an alarming rate!

I'm really not particular when it comes to digital delay pedals, but I do recommend the Danelectro Reel Echo. For gigs, I use a Zoom G2 pedal. I've been using these Zoom pedals since the late 90's and I like them because they're relatively inexpensive and have a good array of effects, as well as a mute for the tuner, which is particularly handy during a gig. The G2 has the usual echo and reverb settings that you can edit to your personal taste. I have four settings that I use regularly: a short slap-back echo, a slightly longer version of the same echo, a tremolo effect, and a very short reverb which is really more of an ambient sound because it just helps to fatten everything out. I use these individually to suit particular songs, but my main setting is the short slap-back echo and I'll use that for 90% of a typical gig.

I also own a couple of Nocturne Brain pedals and highly recommend them. You can find out more at **https:// www.thenocturnebrain.com/**

Strings

When it comes to strings, I use Ernie Ball 10-46 gauge, but swap the B and G strings for a 12 and 18, respectively. I prefer a wound G as it's another element in the overall sound that helps to fatten things up, plus I find them easier to play. I don't play big string bends a great deal, so there's no need to use a lighter gauge than 10's.

For many players, even 10 gauge strings may seem light for a big Gretsch guitar, but there are a couple of tricks I use to keep them in tune. First, I have the Bisgby screwed into the body of the guitar, underneath where the spring sits. This stops the tailpiece moving from side to side, which does happen if you're over enthusiastic with the arm! Secondly, I glue or pin (I prefer the latter) the bridge. This is very important as it means the tailpiece and bridge no longer move around, either individually or together. When there is some slippage, this is the main cause of tuning problems. I understand many players won't be very keen on drilling holes in their expensive or much-cherished guitars, but these two simple steps have solved my tuning issues with a Bigsby tremolo unit.

So, there you have it. I hope that has been of help. My sincere thanks for your support and I do hope you've found this book a help in mastering this iconic style of guitar playing. Happy pickin' and don't let the bop stop!

Darrel Higham

August 2020

www.ingramcontent.com/pod-product-compliance
Lightning Source LLC
Chambersburg PA
CBHW081433090426
42740CB00017B/3289